ZENSHO W. KOPP

The immortality of the true self

The brilliant, all-pervading light of the self-radiating One Mind is your true birthless and deathless nature.

This light shines eternally of itself, completely free of the senses and all phenomena. The true path to liberation is for you to trust in this spiritual light and experience it yourself.

The pure mind, free from birth and death and all thinking, is your true, immortal self. On the other hand, the discriminating intellect is comprised solely of thoughts.

When the thoughts dissolve away in mystical immersion, this restless, discriminating mind vanishes and the true self shines forth.

Zen means returning to the origin of our true essence. The original state of our mind is the reality behind all experiences.

Reaching the original state of the mind and thus becoming free from all limitations is to directly experience the truth of Zen.

Achieve a consciousness that is attached to nothing at all and is empty, like empty space. Free yourself from all of your concepts, whatever they may be.

If you could achieve a state beyond thinking in crystal-clear awareness, you would recognise that the mind's essence is empty.

Only a radiatingly clear mind without any discriminating thought perceives itself.

In order to abide in cheerful and serene reflection of the mind there is nothing more to do than to leave the mind in its natural state.

Perceive your own mind constantly and everywhere, this is the true practice of Zen.

Relative perception discriminates between subject and object, yet awareness of the true self is absolute and needs no object.

Ignorance dissolves when the feeling of duality disappears. Eliminating all ignorance means realising your true self.

You cannot find God externally. Turn your mind inwards and God will appear as pure consciousness – your true, inner buddha-nature.

In their deepest essence, all people are Buddha. This means that we are none other than the One Mind, the eternal, unchanging buddha-essence, the original source of the entire cosmos, beyond space and time.

Just as light casts out the darkness, all identifications and attachments disappear of their own accord as soon as you realise your true being.

All projections and attachments dissolve in the fire of divine love and you are transformed into the pure reality of your true, immortal self.

You need not invoke God's grace, instead just become inwardly open and empty.

The experience of your birthless and deathless true being takes place in absolute silence in the face of the Eternal.

In order to achieve an insight into your true essence, you must transcend everything and not be attached to anything.

Be as vast and open as the heavens and do not cling to the past, present and future. Thus your mind remains in meditation everywhere, free from discriminating thinking.

Your whole life is one single long dream. Awaken from this fascinating spectacle of illusions.

The perfection of wisdom lies in perceiving that nothing in the world is real.

There is no thinker behind the thoughts but instead, the thoughts themselves create the illusion of a thinker.

The thinker with which you identify is nothing more than the sum of the thoughts.

When the experience of transcendental reality flows into you in all its entirety, in an instant it banishes all dualistic thinking and all suffering.

This experience of the brightly shining true nature of your mind means great liberation.

The true self-mind, as the source of everything, pervades and encompasses everything with the radiating magnificence of its own perfection. Everything is filled with divine fullness.

Recognise this fullness of divine being in small things too. Whoever has veritably perceived their true essence will perceive it in the same way everywhere in all things.

The heart of the enlightened one encompasses the entire universe and their consciousness is brightly shining voidness.

They experience their oneness with the Tao, highest reality, in the silence of inner seclusion and are thus in harmony with the all-embracing wholeness of being.

In truth, there is nothing to achieve. It is just a matter of you reaching a silent understanding of your own mind.

Develop a consciousness that attaches to nothing, for nothing is important in the face of the presence of death.

The moment of death is the pinnacle of life. It is the great chance for a person to break through the deceptive nature of all phenomena and awaken from the dream of body, mind and world.

You can only reach liberation from the cycle of birth and death by perceiving the true nature of your mind.

Without turning your attention to the myriad phenomena and whilst remaining free from identifications, uphold the flame of awareness and rest in natural clarity in the sublime, perfect open vastness of the Mind.

Abiding in this relaxed, clear awareness, free from dualistic perception, you will see that phenomena are not perceived as anything concrete but are directly experienced as consciousness.

Make inside to outside and outside to inside, then you will experience your true being everywhere and at all times.

The free, unimpeded action of the wisdom of your original essence is when you neither allow your mind to abide outwardly nor inwardly, when it is free from coming and going and when the attaching mind is eliminated.

Being fulfilled with your true self means being empty of everything. However, being full of everything means being empty of your true self.

The world can add nothing to the inner fullness of whoever is One with God since they already experience consummate fullness of the divine within them.

When you constantly let all thoughts pass by like clouds in the sky and abide within yourself, relaxed in cheerful serenity, then all tension and duality dissolve away.

When you are not fixated but instead are just simply present and are pure awareness, the subject-object tension dissolves and you feel that everything is just Mind.

The true nature of the mind is perfection. It lacks nothing. It requires no correction.

Therefore, abide in Zen meditation in pure, intentionless self-awareness of mind until the mind in its boundless, open vastness is only aware of itself.

In the innermost ground of your being, the boundless eternal vastness of the mind reveals itself.

Thus, merge your breathing with empty space and be absolutely present in the present moment so that you become completely permeated with divine essence.

In the silence of the mind you experience the unity of body, breathing and mind.
In this silence, which is beyond time and space, all duality dissolves.

You cannot find your true, immortal being in the past or in the future. It only reveals itself to you in the timeless eternity of Now.

If you truly wish to experience the reality of your true essence, you must encounter it directly and immerse yourself in the present moment with your entire essence.

For this reason, in Zen practice, it is essential to realise a cheerful, relaxed and empty self-awareness of the mind, so that you constantly experience clarity of mind in the absolute moment of Here and Now.

Meditation is not something that you do but is what you are. Meditation is your true nature. It is the clear, natural state in which the mind abides within itself in silence, serenity and peace.

There is no other way to perceive the truth than to immerse yourself in your innermost ground and experience your true essence.

Through the transformative power of our devotion to and love of the divine, we achieve consummate, inner seclusion of the mind.

Love's ultimate desire is complete dissolution of the lover into radiating divine reality, which is pure love.

The nature of enlightened omni-awareness is pure consciousness and is as empty as boundless space. It is everlasting being, free from birth and death, joy and suffering.

In this experience of pure, enlightened omni-awareness, there are neither objects to observe nor an observer. By virtue of the spontaneous presence of pristine consciousness, there is no goal to be achieved.

The non-attaching mind, which abides nowhere, is the true mind of a buddha. Only your conditioned thinking makes you unfree.

Therefore, let go of your compulsion to think and abide with your consciousness in the direct presence of pure being. Thus you achieve constant peace of mind.

The fundamental nature of the universe is a boundless, vast emptiness, without a single thing for one to grasp.

This original emptiness is the plenitude of divine essence – the reality of your unborn and thus deathless, true being.

The human mind is a prisoner of its self-created, dualistic perception that is bound to objects.

That is why people never look inwards and thus cannot recognise their true, immortal self, which is completely free of all external influences.

You are not your body, for the body with which you identify yourself is just the visible, mental manifestation of your karmic driving forces.

As long as you are still convinced that you are your body that covers your immortal, true self, you will remain bound to the cycle of birth and death.

Zen is the essence and the peak of the whole of Buddhism. It is the direct way of instantly grasping reality, just as it is.

The truth of Zen is free of all opposites. It is beyond yes and no, beyond phenomena and reality.

The crucifixion of Jesus points to the necessity of mystical death. The annihilation of the ego, the delusion of an "I," is the moment of resurrection of the immortal, true self.

When you have achieved relinquishment by forgetting yourself and all things, the boundless expanse of the One Mind will reveal itself to you, as brilliant as a thousand suns.

The world that you experience as solid material in space and time only exists in your consciousness. Anything that can become the contents of our perception is no more than an apparition in our consciousness, without any true essence of its own.

All objects and all phenomena are just apparitions. The One Mind alone, besides which nothing else exists, is the sole reality.

Zen is always immediate and direct. With the greatest of emphasis, it constantly points to your own heart-mind – our immortal buddha-nature.

A Zen master is only ever concerned with clarifying the student's mind so they can experience the original condition of their mind.

A true person of Zen experiences the reality of their true essence in the midst of the world.

Thus, the practice of Zen does not only involve sitting in silence on your meditation cushion but moreover in performing all actions of daily life in a state of awareness and in being completely present in all things.

In the absolute presence of Here and Now, the Eternal reveals itself.

Each moment we live is a divine gift and a unique opportunity for realisation.

If we wish to live a contented, happy life, there is no other way than to live each moment of everyday life in deep awareness.

Everything is the One Mind, beside which nothing else exists. The multiplicity of all phenomena is nothing other than a spectacle on the surface of the mind.

It is like the ripples of the waves that travel across the eternally untouched depths of the ocean.

In the tranquillity of inner silentness the divine word resounds.

The more a person is steeped in the fullness of divine Being, the less he is able through words to express the inexpressible mystery of the Eternal.

In order to reach an inner readiness on the spiritual path for opening your heart to all beings, you must realise selfless concern and compassionate love for all living beings.

By being aware of the all-embracing wholeness of being, in non-discriminating clarity of mind we feel profound reverence and all-encompassing love for all living beings.

You can only achieve great clarity and inner strength by letting go of all thinking and habitual feelings produced by the ego-delusion.

When chains of thought no longer form and instead, each thought arises and once again subsides, without any interaction on your part, you are immersed in boundless perception.

True happiness is only possible through inner peace. For only where no discriminating thinking takes place will consummate peace and blissful joy prevail.

When you perceive this pure awareness, you experience your whole essence with such intensity and inner joy that your entire worldview transforms itself.

When your perception of external things does not blind you, you experience the pure joy of being and transcend the world of appearances.

You will only achieve constant peace when your mind is steadfast and liberated from deceptions, so that a profound and unchanging clarity arises.

The consciousness of all buddhas is a constant awareness of the unblemished, radiating nature of the Mind.

The master is the manifestation of the blessing of all buddhas. To entrust yourself to him means to entrust yourself to them all.

Those who have awakened, experience themselves as the one spaceless and timeless reality, beside which nothing else exists.

Whoever has truly recognised their true essence beyond birth and death will equally recognise it in all things.

Zen is a life without shackles, a life in freedom and is freedom itself. True life in Zen means retaining a non-attaching mind, everywhere and at all times.

Direct, personal experience is everything. There is no other way to liberation than to awaken to your birthless and deathless true essence.

Nothing exists beyond your consciousness. Everything is just a dream, without any reality.

In Zen it is ultimately a matter of seeing clearly and awakening to the point where you have completely awakened. However, as long as you are still dreaming, you are in your self-created dream of birth and death.

When your mind abides in the absolute presence of Here and Now, you are in unison with heaven and earth.

In the powerful silence of non-thinking, in which you uphold the flame of awareness, your mind achieves imperturbability.

If we sincerely wish to experience our true essence, we must leave all philosophical speculation far behind us and turn to our inner source of knowledge.

Only here will that inexpressible mystery reveal itself to us that manifests itself as our immortal, true self beyond all designation.

Impressum

First edition 2023

Original title **"Die Unsterblichkeit des wahren Selbst"**
published by Spirit Rainbow Verlag, Aachen, Germany 2022

All rights reserved. This book, or parts thereof, may not be reproduced in any form without permission. Printed in Germany.

Original idea and design: Verena Kopp
Image editing: Reinhard Zanella
Translation: John Kitching
Typesetting/ Cover design: Reinhard Zanella
Back cover photo: Axel Jung

© 2023, Zensho W. Kopp

Production and publishing:
BoD - Books on Demand, Norderstedt
ISBN: 9783738610598

Zensho W. Kopp, born 1938, is one of the most significant spiritual masters of our present times and teaches a contemporary path to spiritual realisation. The internationally renowned author of numerous Zen books and audio books instructs a large community of students and directs the Zen Center Tao Chan in Wiesbaden, Germany.

Tao Chan Zentrum e.V., Non-profit society, Wiesbaden.
More info at: **www.tao-chan.org**

Twice a month, the Zen Center Tao Chan organises a Zen-evening with a talk by Zen Master Zensho W. Kopp, where guests are welcome to attend. There is also the possibility for asking Zen Master Zensho questions.

Register here for the evening:
www.tao-chan.org/events/events-zen-night.html

Subscribe here for free short talks by Zen Master Zensho W. Kopp:
www.youtube.com/@zencentertaochan/shorts
www.youtube.com/@zencentertaochan

Facebook site for the Zen Center Tao Chan
www.facebook.com/zencentertaochan

Image credits

shutterstock
1. **Von Ilin Sergey** – image number 2808419, 2808420
2. **Von Juli** – image number 26945326
3. **Von KeilaNeokow EliVokounova** – image number 121145263, 121145815, 146553170, 150619109, 169525232, 179144918, 198360890, 234171106, 1154221531, 1536574373
4. **Von WhiteHaven** – image number 309816896, 309816959, 309816968, 309816998, 309819212, 309819215, 309819278, 309819287, 309819299, 390762643, 390762649, 390762709, 390767284, 390767305, 1709464009
5. **Von Nalaphotos** – image number 636797257

Books and audiobooks by Zensho W. Kopp
also available as eBook in ePUB and Kindle format

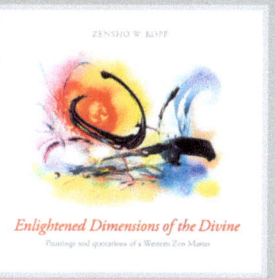

Modern ZEN-ART, Watercolours and sayings of a Western Zen Master.
124 pages, 23,50 €

Enlightened Dimensions of the Divine, Paintings and quotations of a Western Zen Master
140 pages, 10,50 €

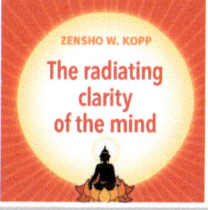

The Flame of Awareness
124 pages

Living in inner fullness
116 pages, 9,80 €

The power of inner quietude
104 pages, 9,80 €

The radiating clarity of the mind
136 pages, 12,95 €

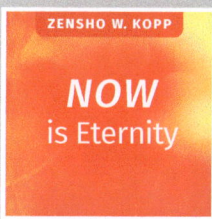
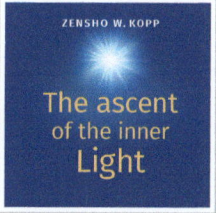

Now is Eternity
114 pages, 9,80 €

The ascent of the inner Light
114 pages, 11,99 €

The mystery of true self-perception
124 pages

Books and audiobooks by Zensho W. Kopp
also available as eBook in ePUB and Kindle format

The ZEN Ox-herding Pictures
The path to Enlightment
212 pages, 9,95 €

True Life Through Zen
Spiritual self-realisation in daily life
140 pages, 11,50 €

Awakening to Your True Self
The Zen way of all-embracing mysticism
140 pages, 11,99 €

Lao-tse Tao Te King
The book of Tao and spiritual force
120 pages, 7,95 €

All publications by Zensho can be found and purchased here:
www.tao-chan.org/zen-master-zensho/books.html

Books and audiobooks by Zensho W. Kopp
also available as eBook in ePUB and Kindle format

The Direct Zen-Way to Liberation
212 pages, 9,95 €

ZEN in daily life
187 pages

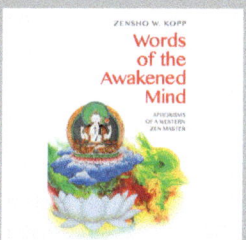

Words of the Awakened Mind
140 pages, 9,95 €

The Freedom of ZEN
216 pages